SECRET HISTORY

CONFLICT IN THE MIDDLE EAST

DAVID ABBOTT

W

FRANKLIN WATTS

First published in 2010 by Franklin Watts

Copyright © 2010 Arcturus Publishing Limited

Franklin Watts
338 Euston Road
London NW1 3BH

Franklin Watts Australia
Level 17/207 Kent Street, Sydney, NSW 2000

Produced by Arcturus Publishing Limited,
26/27 Bickels Yard, 151–153 Bermondsey Street,
London SE1 3HA

Series concept: Alex Woolf
Editor and picture researcher: Alex Woolf
Designer: Tall Tree

A CIP catalogue record for this book is available from
the British Library.

Dewey Decimal Classification Number: 327.1'2'0956

ISBN 978 0 7496 8226 2

Printed in China

Franklin Watts is a division of Hachette Children's
Books, an Hachette Livre UK company.
www.hachettelivre.co.uk

SL000971EN

Picture credits:
Arcturus: 7 (The Map Studio).
Corbis: cover *bottom right* (John A Giordano), 6
(Bettmann), 8 (David Rubinger), 11 (Janet Jarman), 14
(Jeffrey L Rotman), 15 (Stefane Ruet/Sygma), 16 (Ali
Ali/epa), 17 (Ibraheem Abu Mustaf/Reuters), 23
(David Rubinger), 25 (Reuters), 26 (Reuters), 29 (David
Rubinger), 32 (Haim Azulay/Reuters), 34 (Peter
Turnley), 41 (Magnus Johansson/Reuters), 42 (Andy
Aitchison), 43 (Kevin Lamarque/Reuters).
Getty Images: 9, 10 (Chris Bouroncle/AFP), 12 (AFP),
13 (STR/AFP), 18 (Mohammed Abed/AFP), 19 (Abid
Katib), 20 (Brian Hendler), 21 (Yoav Lemmer/AFP), 22
(Joseph Barrak/AFP), 24 (Louai Beshara/AFP), 27
(Digital Globe), 28, 30 (Abid Katib), 31 (AFP), 33
(Mohammed Abed/AFP), 35 (Yoav Lemmer/AFP), 36
(AFP), 37, 38, 39 (Patrick Baz/AFP), 40 (Uriel Sinai).
Shutterstock: cover top left (Huebi); cover *bottom left*
(Jiri Flogel); cover *bottom middle* (Ingvar Bjork); 24
Belgian chocolates (anlad).

Cover pictures: *top left:* the Israeli flag; *bottom left:* the
Palestinian flag; *bottom middle:* a mobile phone; *bottom right:* former Mossad agent, Ben Menash.

Spread head pictures are all from Shutterstock: 6:
Merkava Mark IV Israeli tank (Dmitry Pistrov); 8: satellite (Pinchuk Alexey); 10, 12: sunglasses (Robnroll); 14,
22: headphones (Dmitry Naumov); 16: shovel
(mmaxer); 18: laptop (terekhov igor); 20, 28, 32: rifle
(RCPPHOTO); 24, 30: hand gun (Jiri Vaclavek); 26:
missile (mmaxer); 34: megaphone (MilousSK); 36, 42:
handshake (David Gilder); 38: dynamite (Andrey
Burmakin); 40: barbed wire (Nikita Rogul).

Every attempt has been made to clear copyright.
Should there be any inadvertent omission, please apply
to the publisher for rectification.

CONTENTS

INTRODUCTION

The Middle East is a region covering south-western Asia and northern Africa. Since 1948 the region has been in a state of continual conflict. The major cause of this conflict was the creation of the modern Jewish state of Israel.

David Ben-Gurion, Israel's first Prime Minister, proclaims the founding of the state of Israel, in Tel Aviv, on 15 May 1948.

THE STATE OF ISRAEL

Jews had been settling in the land known as Palestine on the shores of the eastern Mediterranean since the late 1800s. They came to escape persecution in Europe and Russia and because Palestine was the site of the Biblical Jewish state of Israel. The arrival of Jewish settlers caused conflict with the native Palestinian Arabs. The British rulers of

IN THEIR OWN WORDS

Theodor Herzl was the founder of the Zionist movement for the creation of a Jewish homeland in Palestine. He wrote:

Palestine is our unforgettable historic homeland.... The Jews who will it shall achieve their State. We shall live at last as free men on our own soil, and in our own homes peacefully die.

From *Der Judenstaat* (1896)

Palestine struggled to keep the peace and, in May 1948, they decided to withdraw.

THE LONG WAR

The modern state of Israel was created on 14 May 1948. The idea of a Jewish state in the mainly Muslim Middle East angered the Palestinians and the surrounding Arab nations. They were determined to destroy Israel.

The first Arab-Israeli war lasted almost a year and the fragile peace that followed it did not last long. War broke out again in 1956, 1967 and 1973. In between, and ever since, there has been conflict in the region.

The conflict has at times been a conventional war between professional armies. However, for much of the time, it has been unconventional, characterized by guerrilla conflict and terrorism. Much of the activity in this unusual war has gone on secretly. All sides in the conflict have made use of spies, surveillance, double agents, special operations and secret weapons. In this book we will look in detail at this secret war in the Middle East.

CHANGING BORDERS

- During the first Arab-Israeli war, Israel took control of 77 per cent of former Palestine, Jordan took over the West Bank and Egypt occupied the Gaza Strip.
- In the Six Day War of 1967, Israel conquered the West Bank, the Gaza Strip and the Golan Heights (taken from Syria).
- In 2005 Israel withdrew from the Gaza Strip.

ESPIONAGE AND SURVEILLANCE

Israel has made great use of its intelligence agencies to monitor, track down and attack its enemies. It has three main intelligence services: Mossad, Shin Bet and Aman.

Isser Harel was the second director of Mossad, serving from 1952 to 1963.

MOSSAD

Mossad, formed in 1951, is responsible for gathering intelligence from overseas and carrying out covert operations, including paramilitary activities. It has a staff of around 1,200. Most have worked in the Israel Defence Force (IDF). Its main task is collecting intelligence through the use of spies working under cover, or as diplomats.

REUVEN SHILOAH

Reuven Shiloah (1909–59), the first director of Mossad, was born in Jerusalem. Before the 1948 Arab-Israeli War, Shiloah obtained the enemy's invasion plans. In 1949 he persuaded Israel's first prime minister David Ben-Gurion to set up Mossad. Shiloah resigned in 1952 following the collapse of Israel's spy network in Iraq.

SHIN BET

Shin Bet is responsible for Israel's internal security, conducting intelligence gathering and counter-espionage work within Israel. It relies mainly on human intelligence (HUMINT), using informers from the local population to collect intelligence about planned attacks or the location of terrorist leaders.

AMAN

Intelligence-gathering is often concerned with finding out military secrets, so the IDF have their own intelligence service, Aman. With a staff of around 7,000, Aman is responsible for supplying the IDF with the intelligence it needs to conduct military planning and operations.

IN THEIR OWN WORDS

Former Mossad agent Victor Ostrovsky discusses where intelligence comes from:

Between 60 and 65 per cent of all information collected comes from open media; from 5 to 10 per cent from liaison; and between 2 and 4 per cent from ... agents, or human intelligence, but that small percentage is the most important of all the intelligence gathered.

Victor Ostrovsky, *By Way of Deception* (St Martin's Press, 1990)

9

SECRET AGENTS AT WORK

Spies carry out highly dangerous work. They must be able to operate alone in foreign places, blend in, win the trust of their enemies, obtain accurate intelligence and, if necessary, withstand torture.

In 2007 Mohammed al-Attar was found guilty of spying on Egypt for Israel and sentenced to 15 years imprisonment. Al-Attar, who worked in a bank before he was arrested, claims he only confessed because he was tortured.

THE LIFE OF A SPY

A spy's daily routine will vary a lot depending on his or her precise role. Not all spies are regularly exposed to danger; some work in offices, analysing intelligence reports or signals intelligence. Some spies may have other jobs, which they use as a cover for their spying activity. In Mossad, some agents act as 'combatants', gathering intelligence in foreign countries, led by a small core of katsas (case officers). Others work as assassins; both Israeli and Arab secret services have been accused of killing political enemies.

IN THEIR OWN WORDS

Tzipi Livni, a former Mossad spy, recalls:

You're loaded up all the time with adrenaline. Most of the time I was doing strange things normal people never do. I lost all my spontaneity. You must be focused and calculated all the time. Even when I went to the newsagent I would check to see if I had a tail.

www.americanintelligence.us/News/article/sid=5431.html

LEARNING TO BE A SPY

Spy training can be intense, sometimes brutal, and not many people have the necessary qualities to make it through the course. Victor Ostrovsky, who worked as a katsa in the 1980s, claims that a new intake of 30 to 40 katsas is recruited around every three years, from a field of about 5,000 applicants.

Some applicants apply directly; others are approached by Mossad. For katsas there is a lengthy screening process and exhaustive psychological profiling. Those who pass this initial stage are invited to attend a training course at the Midrasha – the Mossad Training Academy based in Tel Aviv.

Spies in Egypt and Syria have been active in Lebanon and the occupied territories, helping to recruit and train new members of terrorist groups such as Hezbollah and Hamas.

KATSA TRAINING

Training a katsa takes three years. Recruits learn vital skills such as how to follow a suspect, how to recognize whether they are being followed and how to use dead letter boxes (see page 14) and secret codes. Katsas will also learn the subtle arts of recruiting informers and creating credible cover stories. All katsas undergo severe physical testing to ensure that they can withstand beating and torture without giving away information. They also learn how to use the Beretta pistol and are trained in a self-defence method called Krav Maga.

DOUBLE AGENTS

Double agents spy for one country or cause while pretending to spy for another. They may have begun as loyal agents working for their original country or organization. In the course of their career, they may have been recruited to the other side through blackmail (the threat to expose a secret), bribery or because they have become disillusioned.

A protester in Jerusalem calls on the United States to free Jonathan Pollard, who is regarded as a hero by many Israelis.

MOUKHARBEL

In 1973 Mossad recruited a Palestinian spy called Moukharbel. Money provided part of his motivation, but he also believed that by working for both Mossad and the Palestinians he would be able to ensure his own safety. He was playing a risky

JONATHAN POLLARD

Jonathan Pollard worked for US Naval Intelligence in the 1980s and passed on details of, among other things, America's global electronic surveillance network to Israel. Pollard gave documents to his Israeli handler at a carwash. The Israeli agent copied the documents using a battery-operated copier fitted beneath his car dashboard. Pollard was arrested in 1987 and sentenced to life imprisonment.

game, however, and in 1975 Moukharbel was killed by the Venezuelan-born, pro-Palestinian terrorist Carlos the Jackal.

ASHRAF MARWAN

Another alleged double agent was Egyptian billionnaire Ashraf Marwan. He approached members of Mossad in 1969, offering them Egyptian state documents. Thereafter he met them in a London safe house, supplying them with information in exchange for money. In April 1973 Marwan warned Israel that Egypt and Syria were planning a surprise attack the following month. This turned out to be incorrect, costing Israel millions of dollars in extra security.

ISMAIL SOWAN

In the late 1970s Ismail Sowan, a Palestinian from the West Bank, witnessed a Palestinian attack on a bus. This made him want to work for the Israelis. He was recruited to Mossad and then, under their orders, he joined the Palestine Liberation Organization (PLO). He spent several years passing on information to Mossad and was involved in the killing of Palestinian cartoonist Naji Al-Ali.

When Marwan warned Israel again of a joint Egyptian-Syrian attack on Yom Kippur (6 October) 1973, Israel did not heed the warning and were taken by surprise when it actually happened. Did Marwan deliberately mislead the Israelis? Was he really working for them or was he an Egyptian double agent? Only the Egyptians know for sure, and they're not saying.

Ashraf Marwan died mysteriously in 2007 after 'falling' from a window in his London flat. A witness saw two men looking out of the window just after Marwan fell, but no arrests have ever been made.

SPYING EQUIPMENT

To carry out their work, modern spies in the Middle East and elsewhere use a wide range of sophisticated equipment, including computers, mobile phones and satellites. Spying is still dangerous, but new technology can make it easier to gather intelligence.

Miniature cameras are small, easy to hide and simple to use.

CAMERAS AND MICROFILM

Often it is too dangerous for a spy to steal a document, so he or she will photograph it instead. Mossad agents use a variety of miniature cameras for this task. They also use a small 'clamper' camera, which allows a lot of documents to be copied very quickly and replaced – one roll of film can take 500 pictures. Syrian agents have used miniature cameras embedded in their wrist watches.

Once intelligence has been obtained, agents can pass it on using invisible ink or 'floater film', a type of microfilm that can be

DEAD LETTER BOXES

Spies sometimes need hiding places where they can leave secret material, such as papers, film or data sticks, so that another agent can collect it without having to meet them. These secret drop-off locations are known as dead letter boxes. They are usually to be found outdoors and may be an inconspicuous box or even a space beneath a rock or a hole in the wall.

In 1998 Mossad agents installed hidden microphones in this basement to eavesdrop on the Iranian delegation to the United Nations, located in the rooms above.

stuck on to envelopes. If they have access to the Internet, information can be transmitted in coded electronic form as images or audio signals.

MOSSAD SPY TOOLS

Spies need to travel quickly and easily under a false name and identity. Mossad has a whole department devoted to the task of manufacturing fake passports from all over the world. Sometimes agents need to break into houses and offices to gain information. Mossad makes master keys – both the old-fashioned variety and modern code and card keys. If agents can make a cast of a key by pressing it into plasticine, Mossad can supply them with an accurate copy.

ASSASSINATION WEAPONS

Mossad agents use the Beretta 0.22 calibre pistol. They use blunt 'dum dum' bullets as these inflict maximum injury. Agents of Kidon – the Mossad department that carries out assassinations – use the Desert Eagle pistol or, when stealth is required, a stiletto dagger. According to US intelligence, Syrian agents have used a 'fountain pen revolver' and an arrow launcher, which can kill without noise at a distance of up to 75 metres.

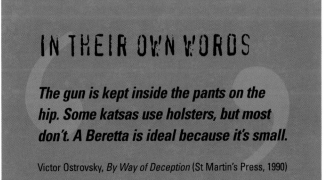

IN THEIR OWN WORDS

The gun is kept inside the pants on the hip. Some katsas use holsters, but most don't. A Beretta is ideal because it's small.

Victor Ostrovsky, *By Way of Deception* (St Martin's Press, 1990)

15

SECRET TUNNELS

Since Israel's withdrawal from the Gaza Strip in 2005, access to the Palestinian-controlled coastal strip has been closely controlled by the IDF and has become a point of conflict between Israelis and Palestinians. The south-western border of the Gaza Strip adjoins Egypt, and Palestinians have dug tunnels along this border through which they smuggle people, cheap goods and weapons into Gaza.

PRICE LIST

According to a report in the *Jerusalem Post*, the price (in US$) of smuggling certain items through the Gaza tunnels is approximately as follows:

- person   1,000
- Kalashnikov rifle   up to 1,000
- single bullet   3

Some 3,000 smuggling tunnels existed on the Egypt–Gaza Strip border in 2008. After Israeli efforts to demolish them during the Gaza War of December 2008–January 2009, only about 150 remained.

HAMAS IN GAZA

The Gaza Strip is controlled by the fiercely anti-Israeli, Palestinian Islamist movement, Hamas. Hamas has launched frequent missile attacks from Gaza on to nearby Israeli towns and villages. Israel has responded by placing the Gaza Strip under a state of siege, controlling its borders and air space and, in January 2009, even invading the territory.

The only border in Gaza that Israel cannot control is the south-western border with Egypt. Most of this border, on the Gaza side, is taken up by the town of Rafah. The town's location makes it an ideal place for building tunnels into Egypt. The tunnels are often started in the basements of residential homes or offices. Great efforts are made to conceal the entrances and exits. The tunnels are usually around 15 metres deep and can be up to 800 metres long.

THE SMUGGLING BUSINESS

Palestinians use the tunnels to smuggle people, food, cigarettes and medicines into the Gaza Strip. Militants also use them to smuggle weapons, including anti-tank and anti-aircraft missiles. For this reason, Israel is anxious to locate and demolish the tunnels.

In December 2009, Palestinians protest against Egypt's proposed construction of an underground steel barrier next to its border with Gaza, to prevent the Palestinians using smuggling tunnels. The barrier will be built beneath this barbed wire.

The tunnels are operated as businesses by prominent Palestinian families such as that of the terrorist Jamal Abu Samhadana (see panel). They cost around US$90,000 to build, but bringing weapons and other goods into the Gaza Strip can make large profits for the owners.

ABU SAMHADANA

Jamal Abu Samhadana, based in Rafah, was the founder of the Popular Resistance Committee, allegedly responsible for missile attacks on Israel. Number two on Israel's list of most-wanted terrorists, he was killed by an Israeli airstrike in 2006.

17

COUNTERING TERRORISM

Since the 1960s, Israel has frequently been targeted by Palestinian terrorist groups. Terrorism has taken the form of suicide bombings, kidnappings, hijackings and assassinations. The intelligence agency responsible for countering terrorism is Shin Bet, also known as Shabak. The motto of Shin Bet is 'unseen shield'.

The militant Hamas leader, Abdel Aziz al-Rantissi, was assassinated in a rocket attack by the IDF in 2004. His car took a direct hit from at least two missiles fired by an Israeli helicopter.

SHIN BET

Since Israel's occupation of the West Bank and the Gaza Strip in 1967, Shin Bet has played a key role in countering terrorist activity by Palestinian militants in the occupied territories. The agency gathers intelligence about Palestinian resistance groups through a network of moles and informers and through the interrogation of terrorist suspects.

MOBILE PHONE BOMB

In 1996 Shin Bet assassinated Hamas's chief bombmaker, Yahya Ayyash. An agent tricked one of Ayyash's friends into giving him a mobile phone rigged with an explosive device. When Ayyash used the phone, the agent detonated it, killing him instantly.

INFORMERS

Much of Shin Bet's intelligence comes from human intelligence (HUMINT). Informers from within the Palestinian community provide intelligence about planned attacks and terrorist groups. Their information has led to the assassination of top militant leaders, including Sheikh Ahmed Yassin and Abdel Aziz al-Rantissi, the founders of Hamas.

INTERROGATION

Another major source of information for Shin Bet is interrogation of prisoners and terrorist suspects. Shin Bet operatives are highly trained in interrogation techniques. In the 1980s and '90s, however, Shin Bet was accused of using torture, including repeated shaking of suspects' upper torsos and the manacling of suspects in painful positions. In one incident, two suspects were executed without trial on the authority of the director.

In 2002 the Israeli parliament passed a law subjecting Shin Bet to closer scrutiny. Since then, Shin Bet has aimed to be more open in its methods, although many of its activities remain shrouded in secrecy.

One of several drawings by Palestinian prisoners depicting torture allegedly carried out by Israeli prison officers. The drawings went on display in a Gaza museum in 2005.

IN THEIR OWN WORDS

Shin Bet started to produce a blog in 2008 in order to help improve the agency's image. One anonymous agent wrote:

We don't work in a basement. We don't spend the day wearing earpieces. And we don't get to have flashing blue lights for our cars. We have to sit in traffic jams like everyone else.

'Israel's Shin Bet launches blog' by Tim Franks. BBC News, 17 March 2008

HOSTAGE RESCUE

Yamam is an elite Israeli police unit specializing in hostage negotiation and rescue. It has about 200 officers, who are organized into teams. The members of each Yamam team live, train and work together, adding to a sense of fellowship and making them a highly effective operating unit.

SPECIALIST SKILLS

Each member of the team is trained in a particular skill useful in hostage situations, so that the team as a whole contains all the resources it needs for a successful operation. Skills include forced entry, sniping, reconnaissance, dog-handling, demolition, bomb disposal and emergency medical treatment.

Yamam officers storm a house.
The occupants had barricaded themselves in and threatened to blow themselves up.

RECRUITMENT

Yamam recruits must have served a minimum of three years in the IDF infantry. Their training lasts a year and includes a 'hell week', claimed to be one of the toughest in the world. Candidates tend to be older than IDF counterterrorism agents. They must demonstrate intelligence, maturity, physical fitness, motivation, stability, decisiveness, teamwork and communication.

IN THEIR OWN WORDS

Yamam was founded in 1975 by Assaf Heffetz. He said of the unit:

Preparation is the key to Yamam's success. When the team goes in, it knows all that can be known about the site and the terrorists. After that, it comes down to fitness and fighting spirit. Luck is not an option.

Source: www.freeman.org/m_online/sep03/baron.htm

Palestinian militants sometimes take hostages in order to force the Israelis to free Palestinian prisoners. These Yamam officers are taking part in an exercise designed to simulate a hostage incident.

OTHER WORK

Since the mid-1990s Yamam has also been used to carry out offensive operations such as dealing with sieges and situations where armed criminals have barricaded themselves into a building and require extraction. Yamam teams have also carried out raids on suspected terrorists in the occupied territories. Members are trained in basic Arabic and given local dress in order to blend in.

Yamam were especially busy during the Palestinian uprising known as the Second Intifada (2000–5). They worked alongside the IDF, carrying out more than 600 operations. They were needed because their training enabled pinpoint accuracy when targeting armed militants in public places full of civilians.

THE MOTHERS BUS

In March 1988, in an incident known as the 'Mothers Bus', Yamam were called in to rescue a bus full of women taken hostage by three Palestinian terrorists. Snipers fired through the windows of the bus, keeping the terrorists occupied until another team stormed the bus and killed them. The operation took a little over a minute and there were just three Israeli deaths – hostages killed by the terrorists.

THE CODE BREAKERS

Successful counterterrorism depends on acquiring accurate intelligence. This can be obtained from human agents (HUMINT) or from intercepted signals (SIGINT). In Israel, the unit responsible for collecting and decoding SIGINT is Unit 8200, a part of the IDF Intelligence Corps.

A masked Lebanese secret service officer shows an electronic transmitter hidden inside an ice cooling container found with Lebanese nationals accused of spying for Israel.

HISTORY

Unit 8200 was set up after the Six Day War in 1967, although its roots go back much further. When Palestine was under British rule (1922–48), the British Army trained Jews to become signals operators and cryptographers (experts in codes). In Israel's early years, these same people listened into the enemy on crudely fashioned radio equipment.

IN THEIR OWN WORDS

Major Arieh Surkis, a founding member of Unit 8200, talks about how things were when he started:

We were very naive, but had extraordinary motivation.... The sentence that epitomizes the feeling we had toward our work was: 'If this isn't ready on time all will be lost'.

Source: dover.idf.il/IDF/English/News/today/2008n/09/0101.htm

LISTENING POSTS

Today, Unit 8200 uses highly sophisticated systems of antennae and receivers to constantly monitor signals transmitted by states such as Egypt, Syria and Iran, as well as by Palestinian groups. Listening posts are set up in the Golan Heights and in and around the West Bank and Gaza Strip. Powerful computers are used to decipher coded messages. The Israelis can even intercept faxes and emails, and listen into mobile phone calls. Unit 8200 also has a section that collects open source intelligence – OSINT – information from Arab newspapers, television and radio.

Both Israel and Egypt use the US-built Hawkeye E-2C electronic reconnaissance aircraft.

FAKE TELEGRAPH POLES

In the 1970s the Israelis listened into the Egyptian military by substituting a real telegraph pole near an Egyptian army base in the Gulf of Suez with a fake pole. Inside the fake pole was a battery-operated transmitter that rebroadcast Egypt's military commands from HQ to listening posts on the Red Sea.

JAMMING ENEMY TRANSMISSIONS

The unit not only gathers intelligence, it also prevents others from acquiring information or from communicating freely. For example, it has been asked by the IDF to jam Palestinian telephone lines to help with the success of military operations.

EGYPT AND SYRIA

The Egyptians and Syrians also use sophisticated listening equipment. The Egyptians have purchased Airborne Early Warning systems from the United States and use satellite technology to transmit sensitive information. The Syrians have built SIGINT stations with help from Iran. They now have four stations: two in the north of the country, one on the Golan Heights and one on the border with Turkey.

SECRET WEAPONS

When working under cover, agents need discreet weapons that won't give away their identity. If they are carrying out assassinations, they need weapons that can enable them to make the killing and get away without attracting attention.

Hamas leader Khaled Mashal evaded a Mossad assassination attempt in Amman, Jordan, in 1997.

ISRAELI WEAPONS

Israeli secret agents are issued with standard weapons such as the Beretta pistol, but use other, less conventional weapons, too. Former Mossad agent Victor Ostrovsky has described how one Kidon operative liked to use a stiletto and a double-bladed claw.

A BUNGLED ASSASSINATION

In 1997 Mossad attempted to murder Hamas leader Khaled Mashal by squirting a lethal nerve toxin into his ear. The agents were arrested in Jordan, however, and international pressure forced Israel to provide an antidote.

DEATH BY CHOCOLATE

The Israelis have allegedly used poison to kill their enemies. In 1978 Palestinian guerrilla Wadi Haddad died a lingering death in an East German hotel. According to journalist Aaron Klein, Haddad was killed by Mossad. The contents of a box of his favourite Belgian chocolates had been coated with a slow-acting, undetectable poison.

This ship, the *Katrine A*, was seized by the Israelis in 2002. The ship was being used by the Palestinians to smuggle Katyusha rockets, mortars and explosives sent from Iran.

PALESTINIAN WEAPONS

Most of the weapons used by Palestinian militants are not sophisticated. It is important, however, that they are acquired and stored in secrecy, to prevent the Israelis from cutting off their supply or destroying their armouries.

Palestinian weapons come from Iran, Syria and from illegal sources in Russia and other countries of the former Soviet Union. Simpler weapons are made by hand in the occupied territories. Chemicals for improvised explosive devices (IEDs) can be produced using detergents or extracted from cosmetics.

SMUGGLING

Weapons from Iran, including rockets, are smuggled into Syria aboard cargo ships and then sent overland to

Palestinian militants in the occupied territories. Weapons are often smuggled into the Gaza Strip through secret tunnels (see page 17). Israeli intelligence monitors shipping movements carefully to prevent such smuggling, while Syrian intelligence attempts to conceal the routes used by the smugglers.

IN THEIR OWN WORDS

We try to never use the same method twice. Our technicians spend all their time devising new ways to kill.

A Mossad source, quoted on www.rense.com/general32/ruth.htm

NUCLEAR WEAPONS

Israel is generally believed to have nuclear weapons. Israeli policy is neither to admit nor deny the fact. Part of the reason is to keep its enemies guessing, so they will hopefully think twice before launching attacks.

Mordechai Vanunu was imprisoned for revealing details of Israel's nuclear weapons programme to the British press. To some he is a hero; to others, a traitor.

OPERATION PLUMBAT

Mossad has played a key role in helping Israel acquire nuclear weapons, as well as identifying the nuclear capabilities of Israel's potential enemies. In 1968 Mossad conducted Operation Plumbat to supply Israel with the uranium necessary for nuclear weapons. Mossad set up a fake company and obtained permission to trade uranium. It arranged for 200 tonnes to be shipped from Antwerp to Genoa. However, during the sea voyage, the cargo was secretly transferred to another vessel and shipped to Israel.

MORDECHAI VANUNU

Mordechai Vanunu was an ex-IDF soldier who worked as a nuclear plant technician at the Negev Nuclear Research Station in the early 1980s. Vanunu became disillusioned and gave details of Israeli nuclear weapons to *The Sunday Times*. A female Mossad operative lured Vanunu to Rome, where he was drugged and kidnapped by agents and smuggled back to face trial in Israel. He was imprisoned for 18 years.

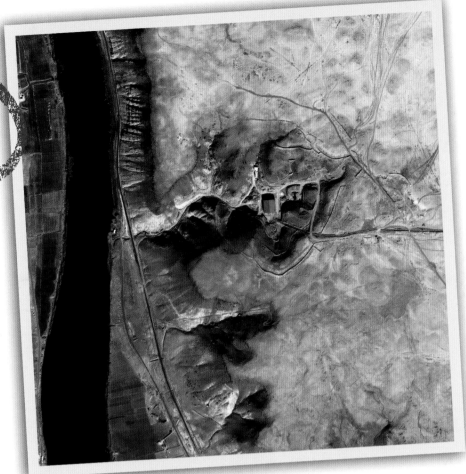

A satellite photo of a site in the north-east of Syria that was bombed by Israeli jets in 2007. The Israelis claimed that the site contained a nuclear reactor capable of producing plutonium for nuclear weapons.

NUCLEAR DEVELOPMENT IN THE NEGEV

Israel's development of nuclear weapons was mainly carried out at a research station in the Negev desert near the city of Dimona. Experts now estimate that Israel has anything between 75 and 400 nuclear warheads. It has the ability to deliver them by missile, aircraft and submarine. Israel is not known to have carried out any nuclear tests.

IRAQ, IRAN AND SYRIA

Other states in the Middle East have tried to obtain nuclear weapons. In the 1980s Iraq attempted to develop nuclear technology with technical help from France, but the Israeli Air Force bombed the plant in 1981. In 2007 the Israelis destroyed a nuclear reactor being built by Syria. Iran is currently developing nuclear weapons technology, despite international criticism.

NETWORK WARFARE

Secret intelligence has played a vital role in Israel's pre-emptive attacks. Some analysts believe that the attack on Syria in 2007 involved intelligence help from the United States. Israeli military intelligence certainly engaged in so-called 'network warfare' during the attack, disrupting Syrian computer systems and causing their air defence network to crash.

OPERATION ENTEBBE

One of the most daring rescue missions in the Middle East conflict was Operation Entebbe in 1976. Palestinian terrorists had hijacked an Air France Airbus flying from Tel Aviv to Athens. The terrorists forced the pilot to fly to Libya and then to Entebbe Airport in Uganda. The terrorists demanded the release of Palestinians held by the Israelis and threatened to kill hostages if their demands were not met.

Lieutenant Colonel Yonatan 'Yoni' Netanyahu, a commander of the Sayeret Matkal, who was killed during the rescue operation at Entebbe.

INTELLIGENCE WORK

Mossad agents went to work, interviewing hostages who had been released by the hijackers. From the information they gained, Mossad was able to give the commandos an accurate picture of the number and location of the terrorists.

SAYERET MATKAL

Sayeret Matkal is an elite commando unit of the IDF and conducts special operations in counterterrorism and reconnaissance. Although the reputation of the unit is legendary in Israel, its activities are shrouded in secrecy and soldiers do not wear any insignia identifying membership of the unit.

Jubilant crowds in Tel Aviv greet the squadron leader of the rescue aircraft used in the Entebbe raid.

THE RESCUE

On the night of the rescue, four Israeli aircraft carrying Sayeret Matkal commandos, landed at Entebbe. Posing as Ugandan leader Idi Amin and his entourage, they drove in a black Mercedes and Land Rover motorcade to the building where the hostages were being held. On entering the building the commandos ordered hostages to stay down as they opened fire on the terrorists.

Hostages indicated a room off the main hall where the remaining terrorists were hiding. Commandos lobbed grenades into the room, killing them. As the hostages were being escorted on board the waiting aircraft, there was a further exchange of fire between commandos and Ugandan soldiers. The rescued hostages were then airlifted to safety.

The entire operation took 53 minutes. One Israeli commando, Lieutenant Colonel Yonatan Netanyahu, was killed and several others were injured. Out of 105 hostages, three died in the crossfire and one, in a Ugandan hospital, was later murdered on Amin's orders. All seven terrorists and around 45 Ugandan soldiers were killed.

IN THEIR OWN WORDS

We are proud not only because we have saved the lives of over a hundred innocent people – men, women and children – but because of the significance of our act for the cause of human freedom.

Chaim Herzog, Israeli ambassador to the United Nations, 1976

ASSASSINATIONS

Since the 1970s, the Israelis have carried out many assassinations of enemy leaders and those involved in terrorist attacks. This policy began as a result of the murder of 11 Israeli athletes by the Black September terrorist group at the 1972 Munich Olympic Games. In response, Israel launched Operation Wrath of God, a covert mission to assassinate those responsible for the massacre.

In 2003 Hamas leader Ibrahim al-Makadma was killed when this car was destroyed by rockets fired from an Israeli helicopter. Three other Palestinians were also killed in the attack.

OPERATION WRATH OF GOD

With the help of Arab informers and friendly European intelligence agencies, a list of targets was drawn up. It was then Mossad's job to locate and kill all of these targets. The assassins had to operate autonomously, so that Israel could, if necessary, deny responsibility. The Israeli government also wanted the killings to send out a message that Israel could strike anywhere at any time, in order to deter future terrorist attacks. Over the next 20 years, secret assassination squads killed around 35 people in Europe

THE LILLEHAMMER AFFAIR

The Lillehammer Affair was an assassination attempt that went wrong. Mossad agents killed a Moroccan waiter called Ahmed Bouchiki, mistaking him for the leader of the Black September group. Five agents were convicted of murder by the Norwegian authorities.

Israel's assassination policy is controversial and has attracted criticism. Israeli attorney general Elyakim Rubinstein attempted to justify it as follows:

The laws of combat which are part of international law, permit injuring, during a period of warlike operations, someone who has been positively identified as a person who is working to carry out fatal attacks against Israeli targets, those people are enemies who are fighting against Israel...

Ha'aretz, 12 February 2001

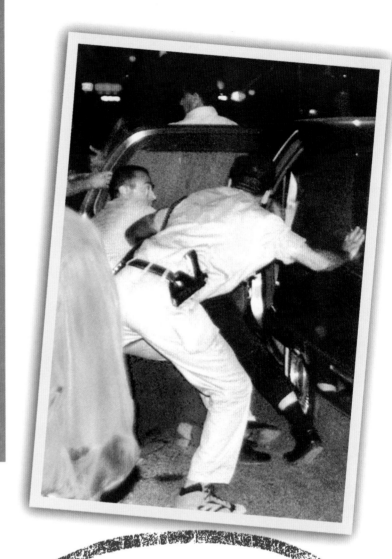

Security agents bundle Israeli premier Yitzhak Rabin into a car after he was shot by an extremist Jewish gunman during a peace rally. The gunman, Yigal Amir, was later sentenced to life imprisonment.

and the Middle East suspected of involvement in the Munich Massacre.

POLITICAL ASSASSINATIONS

The Middle East conflict is littered with the assassinations of political leaders. Anwar Sadat, the Egyptian leader who made peace with Israel in 1979, was killed for this 'betrayal' by Islamists in 1981. In 2005 Rafiq Hariri, the prime minister of Lebanon, was killed by a car bomb. A subsequent investigation pointed to Syrian involvement.

Israel has suffered assassinations of its own. In 1995 Israel's prime minister

Yitzhak Rabin was shot dead by Yigal Amir, a right-wing Orthodox Jew, enraged by Rabin's signing of the Oslo Accords, a 1993 peace treaty with the PLO. In 2001 Israeli tourism minister Rehavam Ze'evi was killed by a Palestinian assassin.

GUERRILLA TACTICS

Although battles between conventional forces occurred regularly in the Middle East between 1948 and 1973, since then the conflict has been one of 'asymmetric warfare', with Israel's well-equipped, modern army fighting against smaller guerrilla forces.

This house in Kiryat Shemona in northern Israel has been damaged by a rocket launched by Hezbollah.

ASYMMETRIC WARFARE

Although small in size and population, Israel is a wealthy, industrialized nation. It has allies in the Western world – especially the United States – that supply its armed forces with the most up-to-date weapons and armour.

By contrast, the Arab militant groups ranged against Israel, such as Hamas, Fatah and Hezbollah, are smaller in number, poorer and have far fewer

HEZBOLLAH ROCKETS

Arab militant groups obtain their weapons from Syria, Iran, Russia and China. In the 2006 Lebanon War between Israel and Hezbollah (a Shi'a Muslim Islamist group based in Lebanon), Hezbollah fired over 4,000 Syrian-made Katyusha rockets at northern Israel at a rate of more than 100 a day, hitting over a dozen cities and many smaller settlements.

resources. To try to overcome this disadvantage, these groups have adopted guerrilla tactics. They avoid pitched battles and instead conduct surprise attacks, rapid raids and ambushes. They attack enemy forces with rockets, bombs and booby traps.

BOOBY-TRAPPED GAZA

Prior to Israel's invasion of the Gaza Strip in January 2009, Hamas and their allies booby-trapped many homes, offices and other buildings with bombs. They placed bombs in TV satellite dishes, next to petrol stations, in mosques and even inside mannequins placed at the windows of houses. Once the invasion began, Hamas used home-made improvised explosive devices (IEDs) to attack IDF soldiers, tanks and armoured personnel carriers.

Hamas militants prepare an IED in Rafah in the Gaza Strip. Since 2009 Hamas bomb-makers have started to adopt the methods of al-Qaeda experts in Afghanistan. Their bombs have been found to contain tungsten, making them much more powerful.

BLENDING IN

Hamas militants wore civilian clothes to confuse the invaders. Israel later accused Hamas of deliberately placing its forces in densely populated areas. This made it harder for the IDF to avoid killing civilians, thereby attracting condemnation from the rest of the world.

IN THEIR OWN WORDS

During the 2008–9 Gaza War, Palestinian guerrilla groups put aside their differences and worked together:

Everybody helps everybody else with regards to food, weapons, and first aid. For everybody's goal is the same and their compass is pointing in the same direction, and that is to drive out the occupation and defeat them....

Abu Ahmed of the al-Quds Brigades, the military wing of Palestinian Islamic Jihad

PROPAGANDA

Propaganda is the organized and deliberate attempt to control news and information in order to persuade people to think or act in a certain way. It has been used by all sides in the Middle Eastern conflict. Each government and group has issued propaganda to reassure their own citizens or supporters, as well as to gain the support and sympathy of the world at large.

HISTORIC CLAIMS

Propaganda has played a major part throughout the history of the conflict, and even colours the way that history is now portrayed. During the violent birth of Israel, hundreds of thousands of Palestinians fled, ending up in refugee camps in the West Bank and Gaza Strip. The Palestinians claim they fled because they were expelled and, in some cases, massacred by Israeli forces. The Israelis say they left of their own accord or were encouraged to leave by neighbouring Arab states.

Hamas members spray-paint a mural in Rafah in the Gaza Strip. Murals boost Palestinian morale and provide an alternative to Israeli accounts of the conflict.

WARTIME PROPAGANDA

During wars and invasions, when the military and paramilitary forces of each side go into action, so do their propaganda machines. In the Gaza War of 2008–9, Hamas accused the IDF of firing on civilian buildings such as hospitals, mosques, schools and UN facilities. The IDF countered by accusing Hamas of using 'civilian shields' – deliberately hiding out in buildings used by civilians.

IN THEIR OWN WORDS

The IDF distributed leaflets among Gaza residents prior to the 2009 invasion:

Rocket launchers and terror elements are a danger to you and your families. If you want to help, all you have to do is call this number and state the location of the rocket launchers and terror cells operating in your area…. You can still prevent disaster. Do not hesitate!

www.haaretz.com/hasen/spages/1054916.html

PSYCHOLOGICAL WARFARE

Psychological warfare, or psyops, is similar to propaganda, but it attempts to scare or demoralize the enemy. The Israelis have made use of psyops in their counterterrorism operations. For example, they have published obituaries of living Palestinian militant leaders, indicating that they are about to be killed. During the Gaza War, Hamas tried to demoralize the Israelis, sending Hebrew text messages to Israeli citizens warning: 'Rockets on all cities, shelters will not protect you'.

35

DIPLOMACY AND SECRECY

Secret talks have been a recurrent feature of the Middle East conflict. Politicians often prefer to negotiate in secret because they do not want to be seen to be talking with terrorists or making concessions to the enemy. Neither do they want the other side to know their negotiating tactics.

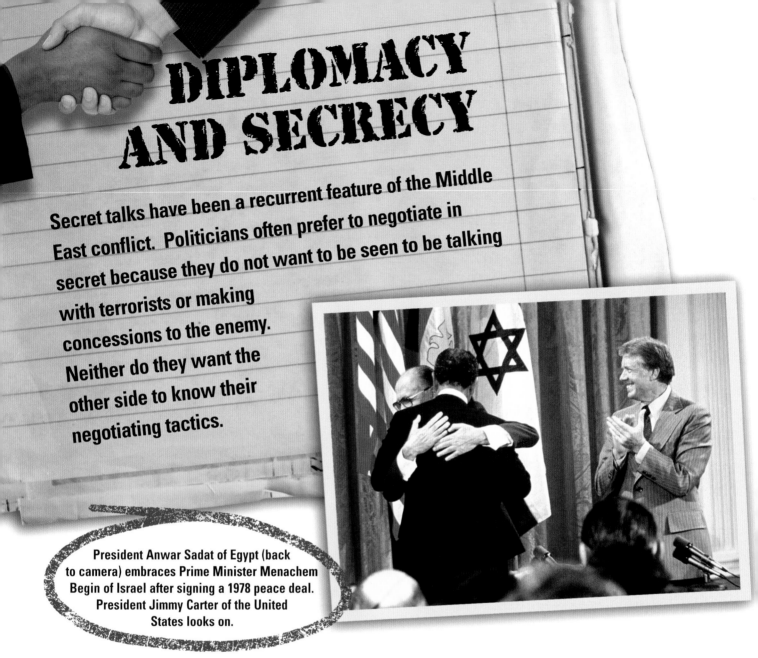

President Anwar Sadat of Egypt (back to camera) embraces Prime Minister Menachem Begin of Israel after signing a 1978 peace deal. President Jimmy Carter of the United States looks on.

CAMP DAVID

Before the 1978–9 Camp David peace talks between Egypt and Israel, Mossad bugged the offices of Arab ambassadors and leaders in the United States. By listening in to their discussions, Mossad learned that the PLO was likely to recognize Israel's right to exist and this enabled Israeli diplomats to drive a hard bargain with President Sadat of Egypt.

In 1979 Mossad found out that the US ambassador to the United Nations, Andrew Young, who was openly critical of Israel, had secretly spoken with a member of the PLO, then considered by many countries to be a terrorist organization. Young was forced to resign and the Israelis were able to continue negotiations with Egypt with a powerful opponent out of the way.

THE OSLO TALKS

Secret talks in Oslo, Norway, in 1993 led to the Oslo Accords, a historic first agreement between Israel and the PLO. The Norwegian government ensured the meetings were kept secret by holding them in a research institute. In this neutral and private setting, the Israeli and Palestinian negotiators could avoid the media spotlight and had the freedom to try out different bargaining positions without fear of criticism at home.

US ambassador Richard Holbrooke speaks privately with Palestinian president Mahmoud Abbas at a conference in 2008. Both sides find it easier to make peace deals if the details are kept private.

IN THEIR OWN WORDS

Ahmed Qurei, PLO representative at Oslo, said:

Any hint of media attention would have ruined the possibility that a new channel might bring a fresh and open mind to the Israeli-Palestinian confrontation. We kept to a bare minimum the number of persons involved in the channel, and the secrecy we observed was in the end, I am sure, one of the elements which led to a positive outcome.

From Oslo to Jerusalem: The Palestinian Story of the Secret Negotiations by Ahmed Qurei (I B Tauris, 2008)

REASONS FOR SECRECY

In 1994 Jordan signed a peace treaty with Israel, a move that upset some of Jordan's Arab neighbours. Syria secretly warned Jordan not to sign the treaty, but did not want to be seen to be obstructing movements towards peace. The Jordanian government had to negotiate through backchannels and avoid upsetting its own population, many of whom were hostile to Israel.

37

TERRORIST ATTACKS

Terrorism is the use of violence against civilian targets to achieve a political aim. Palestinian militant groups such as Hamas, Fatah and Palestinian Islamic Jihad have often used terrorist tactics during the conflict with Israel. Palestinian supporters claim that Israel has used 'state terrorism' in its attacks on Palestinians.

A member of the Black September terrorist group appears on a balcony outside the Israeli Olympic team's headquarters during a stand-off with police at the 1972 Munich Olympic Games. Eleven hostages died in the two-day incident.

Palestinian militants have used different forms of terrorist violence including hijackings, bus bombings and suicide bombings. These types of attacks are intended to:

- maximize panic and fear among the Israeli public.

- gain the attention of the world's media, thereby publicizing the Palestinian cause.

- provoke the Israeli government into disproportionate actions that will alienate world opinion.

Palestinian groups hope that a sustained campaign of terrorist attacks will eventually force Israel into making political concessions. In the late 1960s and the 1970s their chief weapon was hijacking airliners. Since the 1990s it has been suicide bombings.

THE FIRST SUICIDE ATTACKS

The first Palestinian suicide attack occurred in July 1989. A member of Palestinian Islamic Jihad boarded an Israeli bus and pulled the steering wheel, driving the bus into an abyss and killing all 16 people on board. The first suicide bombing was carried out by a Hamas militant in April 1993. He detonated his bomb-laden car between two buses, killing two, including himself, and wounding 21.

The aftermath of an early Palestinian suicide attack in December 1993: a suicide bomber drove this stolen vehicle, packed with explosives, into a group of Israeli soldiers, killing himself and injuring a soldier.

Suicide bombings grew even more frequent during the Second Intifada (2000–5). Targets included buses, IDF checkpoints, shopping malls, restaurants, discos and Jewish settlements in the occupied territories.

In some cases, women and children have been used as suicide bombers because they are less likely to arouse suspicion. In March 2005, near Nablus, an Israeli border guard found a bomb in the schoolbag of a 12-year-old boy. The lives of the guard and the boy were saved only because the remote control device set to detonate the bomb failed to work.

IN THEIR OWN WORDS

Suicide is forbidden by Islamic scripture. Yet this has not prevented some Muslim clerics from attempting to justify 'martyr operations' (suicide bombings):

The martyr operation is the greatest of all sorts of Jihad in the Cause of Allah. A martyr operation is carried out by a person who sacrifices himself, deeming his life less value than striving in the Cause of Allah, in the cause of restoring the land and preserving the dignity.

Sheikh Yusuf al-Qaradawi, quoted on www.islamonline.net

HOSTAGES AND PRISONERS

The taking of hostages and political prisoners has been a major feature of the Middle East conflict. Israel has imprisoned many Palestinians for alleged militant activities. Palestinian groups have seized Israelis and held them hostage. Both sides have used hostages and political prisoners as bargaining chips in negotiations and both have been criticized for human rights abuses on this issue.

Israelis carry banners commemorating the capture and deaths in 2006 of Israeli soldiers Ehud Goldwasser and Eldad Regev. Their bodies were returned in exchange for the release of Hezbollah fighters.

TAKING HOSTAGES

Palestinian militant groups view the taking of hostages as a legitimate tactic that can give them an advantage in an unequal war. To foil Israeli rescue teams, Palestinian groups take great care to keep the whereabouts of hostages secret.

In 1994 Nachshon Wachsman, an off-duty soldier, was taken hostage and died in a rescue attempt by Sayeret Matkal. In 2006 two IDF solidiers were captured by Hezbollah guerrillas in an ambush and

On 9 January 2007, Abu Mujahed, a spokesperson for the captors of Gilad Shalit, said of the hostage:

We have managed to keep the soldier in captivity for six months and we have no problem keeping him for years. Our goal is to put pressure on the Israeli government to release our prisoners.

Palestinian prisoners released from an Israeli prison flash victory signs from a bus window in Bethlehem in 2004. On that occasion, Israel freed 400 Palestinians and 35 others in exchange for the bodies of four Israelis.

later killed. In the same year, Gilad Shalit, an IDF corporal in the Armor Corps, was taken prisoner. His captors have asked for the release of 1,000 Palestinian prisoners in exchange for Shalit.

PRISONER EXCHANGES

Israel has traditionally placed a very high value on the lives of its citizens and has often been willing to release large numbers of Palestinian prisoners in exchange for a few Israeli hostages. In 1985 Israel released 1,000 Palestinian prisoners in exchange for three Israelis. Israel has also been willing to release Palestinian prisoners in pursuit of peace. As part of the Wye River Memorandum, an agreement between Israel and the Palestine Authority in 1998, Israel released around 500 prisoners.

PALESTINIAN PRISONERS

Israel has imprisoned large numbers of Palestinians. Around one-fifth of the population has spent some time in an Israeli jail since 1967. In March 2008 over 8,400 Palestinians were held in Israeli prisons, of which 790 were being held without charge. Many of these were women and minors. The Ben-Porat report (1997), commissioned by the Israeli government, revealed that torture has been used on Palestinians held in Israeli prisons.

CONCLUSION

The recent history of the Middle East does not give much grounds for optimism that the current conflict will be quickly or easily resolved. Periodic moves towards peace have been followed by sudden outbreaks of renewed violence. On both sides there is a legacy of suspicion and bitterness that will not be easily overcome.

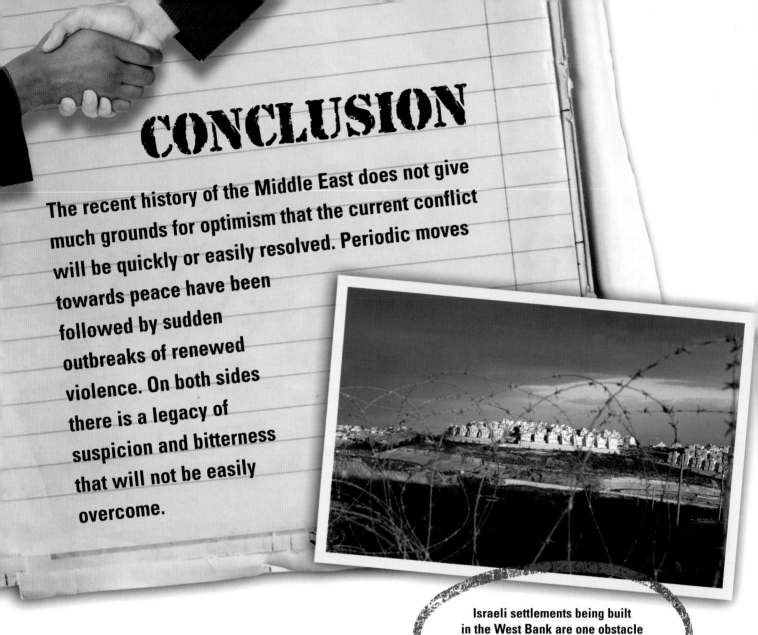

Israeli settlements being built in the West Bank are one obstacle to reaching a peace settlement in the Middle East.

THE CONTINUING WAR

Alongside the ongoing battles between Israel and the Palestinians, the secret war will also continue and grow ever more sophisticated. Israel is likely to persist with its undercover war against the militants. It will make use of the latest satellite surveillance technology to spy on neighbouring states. Most urgently of all, it will be watching Iran and that country's development of nuclear weapons.

Iran and Syria will continue to arm and train Palestinian and Hezbollah militants for as long as it suits them to do so. The Palestinians for their part will continue to wage guerrilla warfare and launch terrorist attacks against Israel unless a peace deal can be negotiated that satisfies them.

US President Barack Obama watches as Israeli prime minister Binyamin Netanyahu (left) and Palestinian president Mahmoud Abbas shake hands in September 2009. Obama supports the idea that the conflict can best be solved by creating two states: one for the Israelis and one for the Palestinians.

The eventual solution to the conflict will be political. But in order to get the political leaders to reach agreement, much secret diplomacy will need to take place first. This has happened before and has produced some surprising successes, such as the treaties between Israel and Egypt in 1979, and Israel and Jordan in 1994. There is always the hope that through patient, behind-the-scenes efforts, peace will eventually come to the Middle East.

INTELLIGENT TALKS

During peace negotiations, both sides desire information their opposite numbers would rather keep hidden. They need accurate information about their opponents' strengths and weaknesses in order to negotiate from a position of strength. How firm is their support among the public? How strong or well-trained are the forces at their disposal? They may also wish to keep their own strengths and weaknesses hidden from the enemy. In all these tasks the intelligence agencies play a vital role.

TIMELINE

1948 Zionist leaders declare the founding of the state of Israel.

1948–9 War between Israel and its neighbouring Arab states.

1951 Mossad is founded.

1967 Six Day War – Israel captures the Gaza Strip, the West Bank and the Golan Heights; Unit 8200 is set up.

1968 Operation Plumbat: Israel obtains nuclear material.

1972 The Munich Massacre – 11 Israeli athletes are murdered by Black September terrorists at the Olympic Games in Munich.

1973 Yom Kippur War – Egypt and Syria launch a joint surprise attack on Israel.

1975 Yamam is founded.

1976 Operation Entebbe – Israeli commandos rescue Jewish hostages held by Palestinian terrorists at Entebbe Airport, Uganda.

1979 Israel and Egypt sign a peace treaty.

1982 Israel invades Lebanon.

1986 Mordechai Vanunu leaks news of Israel's nuclear capability.

1987–93 First Intifada.

1993 The Oslo Accords between Israel and the PLO are signed in Washington.

1995 Israeli Prime Minister Yitzak Rabin is assassinated.

2000–5 Second Intifada.

2006 Lebanon War between Israel and Hezbollah; Corporal Gilad Shalit taken hostage.

2007 Israelis destroy Syrian nuclear reactor.

2008–9 Gaza War – Israel invades the Gaza Strip.

44

GLOSSARY

asymmetric warfare Warfare between opponents who are unequally matched.

counterterrorism Military or political activities intended to combat or prevent terrorism.

cryptography The study or analysis of codes and coding methods.

dead letter box A place where a message or other item can be left in secret by one person and collected later by another, so that the two people do not meet.

Hamas A militant Islamist organization whose goal is an independent Palestinian state on land currently occupied by the state of Israel.

Hezbollah A Shi'a Islamist political and paramilitary organization based in Lebanon.

IDF (Israel Defence Force) The ground, air and naval forces of Israel.

intelligence Information, often secret, about an enemy's forces and plans.

intifada An Arab word usually translated into English as 'uprising'.

Islamist Someone who follows a strict form of Islam based on a literal interpretation of the Qur'an.

katsa A field intelligence officer in Mossad. He or she collects information and runs agents.

Kidon (Hebrew: 'bayonet') A section of Mossad responsible for assassinations and kidnapping.

martyr A person prepared to die for his or her religious beliefs.

microfilm A continuous roll of film containing photos of documents at a greatly reduced size.

militant A person who is active in defence or support of a cause, often to an extent that causes conflict with other people or institutions.

Muslim A follower of Islam, the religion founded by the Prophet Mohammed.

nuclear weapon Bombs or missiles that release nuclear energy to create a massive explosion.

Orthodox Jews Jews who believe in the literal truth of the Torah (Jewish holy book) and follow its laws strictly.

Palestinian Islamic Jihad A militant Palestinian terrorist group created in 1979 and committed to the creation of an Islamic state in Palestine.

paramilitary Describing a military force that is not part of a regular army.

PLO (Palestinian Liberation Organization) An organization, founded in 1964, that represents the Palestinian people. It is an umbrella organization for a number of different groups, including Fatah and the Popular Front for the Liberation of Palestine (PFLP).

psychological profiling A means of examining and testing the personality and traits of someone to see if he or she is capable of, for example, doing a particular job.

reconaissance Exploration of an area to gain information about an enemy.

safe house A secure location suitable for hiding or meeting with witnesses, agents or other persons perceived as being in danger.

surveillance Close observation of a person or group.

terrorism The use of violence against civilian targets to achieve political ends.

uranium A radioactive metallic element. Certain forms of uranium are used to manufacture nuclear weapons.

Zionism A political movement that aimed at establishing a national homeland for the Jewish people in Palestine.

FURTHER INFORMATION

BOOKS
Atlas of Conflicts: The Arab-Israeli Conflict
by Alex Woolf (Franklin Watts, 2004)

Causes and Consequences: The Arab-Israeli Conflict
by Stewart Ross (Evans Brothers, 2004)

Questioning History: The Arab-Israeli Conflict
by Cath Senker (Wayland, 2008)

Timelines: The Arab-Israeli Conflict
by Cath Senker (Franklin Watts, 2007)

Troubled World: The Arab-Israeli Conflict
by Ivan Minnis (Heinemann Library, 2001)

WEBSITES
english.aljazeera.net
Al Jazeera – the news organization based in Doha. The website includes a history of Palestine.

www.mideastweb.org
MidEast Web Gateway is run by volunteers from both sides of the conflict.

www.moi.gov.ps/En/?page=6336570536025000 00
The Website of the Palestinian Ministry of the Interior of the Palestinian National Authority.

www.shabak.gov.il/english
The website of Israel's internal security agency, Shin Bet.

INDEX

Page numbers in **bold** refer to pictures.